IRON MAN OF THE HOH

IRON MAN OF THE HOH

NELSON BENTLEY

COPPER CANYON PRESS

Most of these poems appeared originally in *A Day at North Cove* (Raven's Mask Press chapbook), *Grayland Apocalypse* (Bonefire Press chapbook), *Mill Mountain Review*, *Northwest Review*, and *Pacific*.

SPECIAL THANKS TO:
Centrum Foundation, Fort Worden State Park, Port Townsend, Washington, where Copper Canyon is Press-in-Residence; and for a grant which in part made possible the publication of this book, the National Endowment for the Arts, a federal agency.

ISBN 0-914742-17-5

Printed in the United States of America

Illustration: Dana Wylder
Photo: Greg Gilbert

Copper Canyon Press
Box 271
Port Townsend
Washington 98368

CONTENTS

For Beth, Sean, and Julian

Ediz Hook Apocalypse

In the August when the Wizard of Oz resigned,
I drove Sam Abelson, my ancient Chevrolet,
Past the Blue Moon, Roethke's second home;
A voice floated from near the weathered sign,
"Moose! Moose! Go to Ediz Hook!"
Looking up, I saw Roethke riding on a bear
Which had six wings and eyes in its ears and tail.
They flew beside me along 45th,
Ted waving a Guinness Stout and calling,
"Rejoice, Moose; the great and terrible Oz

Zigzags no more." I stopped at the Roosevelt Way
Traffic light, as the bear circled back
Toward the Blue Moon, but I heard Roethke add,
"Meet us Wednesday at the Edmonds ferry."
It proved to be an unusual voyage:
The bear and Roethke did a vigorous Charleston
On the *Elwha*'s deck, as God is my witness.
Ahead, the Brothers were snowcapped in blue mist
Over Kitsap's wooded slopes. With a long and two
Short toots, we were bumping the tarred pilings.

For the sixty miles to Port Angeles,
The bear and Roethke were soaring and flapping
A hundred yards ahead of Sam Abelson.
Sometimes I heard Ted's growling baritone
Reciting his unpublished poem on Nixon,
Which he'd read once in Michigan in 1960,
Or a short burst of "We're off to see the Wizard."
At times the bear would have a Guinness Stout.
Ted stopped once at the Sequim tiger farm
To look for William Blake, but otherwise

We went straight past the blue bays and forests
To Ediz Hook, which curls into the Strait

Of Juan de Fuca. Ted growled, "Stop right here,
By the Bert Thomas monument." From that point,
Thomas swam to Victoria in 1955.
Great swells were rattling the flat circular rocks
That lie all along the Hook. Thousands of logs,
Roots and stumps of the Klallam forests
Lay tangled above the kelp, between the Crown
Zellerbach paper mill and the Coast Guard.

A strange figure, seated on a Douglas Fir stump,
Gazed over the strait. He wore a stovepipe hat,
And drank from a flask every sixty seconds;
His luminous nose made him resemble a buoy.
Ted climbed off the bear and ambled, swaying,
Slowly toward the stump. "Well, William Claude,
You old scalawag," he grunted, "has Tricky Dick
Come in sight?" Fields jumped, and adjusted his hat.
"Ah, Theodore! Friend of the field mouse.
Behold, a glint of glass among the breakers."

An Old Crow bottle the size of a small yacht
Tossed slowly toward us underneath the smog.
Fields climbed from the stump, singing under his breath,
"When the horse flies take wing in Cincinnatti,"
And offered his flask to the bear, who declined.
The bottle landed, thunk, on the flat stones,
Neck resting on the stump. Inside stood Nixon,
With a Quaker State Motor Oil can on his head,
And Ziegler, in an alligator skin coat.
The crow on the label kept saying "Nevermore."

At that moment, Robert Frost came flapping in
From Hurricane Ridge, on a four-winged Morgan.
Roethke said, "Ziegler looks like Boris Karloff
After a heavy meal." "Or," said Fields, "possibly
An infuriated Buick." Frost added,
"Maybe he'll say *Casey at the Bat*."

"When they floated past Cape Flattery," said Fields,
"A Makah maiden, resembling Pocahontas,
Held up a sign saying 'Keep us apart'."
Gulls dipped and circled through the hazy smoke

From Crown Zellerbach; behind Port Angeles
The Olympics lifted countless blue snowed summits
Over a reddish smog. Frost, eating an apple,
And feeding one to the Morgan, remarked dryly,
"I don't notice any change in Old Stonewall.
Do you suppose he ever read 'Mending Wall'?
I keep thinking of Kennedy's inauguration:
'The greatest vote a people ever cast'."
Roethke growled, "Dick thinks it's the good ship Lollypop,
But it's one of the seven vials of the Wrath of God."

"Let's play Nixon's Revelation," said Fields. "This stump
Will be the Oval Office. I'll be The President.
Piled on the stump are 42 flat rocks,
Each bearing the Presidential Seal."
Roethke climbed onto the stump, saying gruffly,
"I'll play the part of The Faithful Dog."
Frost stood behind Fields and to his left,
And commented, "I'm Abe Lincoln's photograph."
"The President," said Fields, "wishes to introduce
His trusted dog, King Nebuchadnezzar,

Who has bitten six thousand Press representatives
In the interests of National Security.
These 42 rocks each contain six words
Carved by the Finger of God. They are final proof
Of The President's innocence. This has been done
By the Great Zeal of the Lord, from Zion, through Ziegler."
Then Roethke howled like the Hound of the Baskervilles,
Frost fanned himself with a crab skeleton,
And the 42 Presidential Seals
Plunged in the Strait and swam for the open ocean.

Roethke said, "That was the spit and image, Bill,
Every bit as good as *The Bank Dick*."
"Well," said Frost, "let's shove him off. Should the bottle
Be christened?" Roethke poured a Guinness Stout
Over the bottleneck and growled, "I dub you
The Walloping Window Blind. You will float
Our coastal waters seventy years, to warn
All generations of Dick's arrogance."
Fields added, "You will spend the Fourth of July,
1976, cruising the Potomac."

The bear, the Morgan, Frost and Roethke danced
On the driftwood firs; gulls circled above the bottle
As it headed toward the Pacific. Fields tipped
His hatbrim to shade his eyes, and proclaimed,
"The seventy moons of Nixon are no more.
Whenever he tries to escape from the bottle,
A host of angels will sing 'Seventy more moons'."
Among the gull cries, out on the smoggy strait,
The croak of the crow on the label was perfectly clear:
"Nevermore. Nevermore. Nevermore."

August 1974

The Biezk Brothers Garage

Much of my meditation by the age of ten
Had occurred in the Biezk Brothers Garage,
Where my father and I wandered among spark plugs,
Oil pits, rusty radiators, to the clang
Of hammers banging out dented fenders,
And the Biezks wandered greasily about,
Grinning like sooty Grendels from the fens,
Their grimy rears and legs protruding from Reos,
Packards, Model T's, Marmons and Dodges,
In a chaos of honks and patched inner tubes.

There I learned I was a 20th century child.
Many main roads were still dirt and gravel,
Down which buggies moved to a slow trot;
The barns in back of our house still held hay
And the ghosts of horses, but my father bought
His first automobile before I was born.
The Biezk Brothers Garage was in Rough And Ready,
A crossroads between the Middlebelt Air Field
And Stark. Amid their tail pipes, pistons, alcohol,
And carburetors, I entered the Machine Age.

And so I was prepared for my first collision.
On a Sunday morning in May, a year before
The stock market crash, we left the Plymouth
Presbyterian Church in our Studebaker,
My father and mother in front, Margaret
And I in back, and chose Ann Arbor Trail,
A crooked dirt road my father had travelled
Since a boy. The fields were full of Holsteins,
Wild carrot, black-eyed Susans, apple blossoms,
The shaded road lined with maple and elm.

Rounding a curve, we saw a Model T
Crawling in zigzags at 5 miles an hour,

Going alternately up the sandy banks
On both sides of the road, followed by
A small zigzag cloud of dust. "Jee-rusalem,"
My father said, "it's that son of a sea cook,
Charley White, soused again." He began to match
Zigs with Charley's zags, the Studebaker
Crisscrossing the center line of horse manure.
It was like Gary Cooper coming step by step

To a shootout in the Old West. I think
We would have missed him, but he double-zagged.
His Model T tilted from the sand bank
And came to rest, gently as a dandelion,
At a 20 degree angle on the Studebaker;
I heard the lowing of Holsteins, squirrel chatter,
And the harsh cries of a puzzled bluejay.
Clambering out of his now upper door,
Charley shuffled through sand like Lawrence
Of Arabia, saying, "Whatsh the idea, G-George?

You're d-driving on the w-wrong shide of the r-road."
By luck, two Wayne County Sheriff's officers
Drove up and gazed about like Sherlock Holmes.
Up the road, as far as the eye could see,
Model T tracks were looping up the sandbanks.
"Offisher," said Charley, "You should've sheen ol' George
Going b-back and f-forth like Red G-Grange. Do you
Shupposh he'sh had shomthing to drink shomwhere?"
They put handcuffs on Charley and shoved him in
Their car. He climbed quickly out the other side,

And wove back, protesting, followed by a trail
Of dust. "Now you know me, G-George. Jusht tell 'em
I'm shober ash a j-judge. Tell theshe sheriffsh,
You were c-coming zhigzhag, like a m-mother b-bird
P-protecting her n-nesht. That ol' Shtudeb-baker
Looked like a shee-shaw." They shoved Charley back

In their car. He immediately climbed out
The other side, saying, "You know me, G-George.
Tell 'em to t-take theshe cuffsh off and p-put 'em
On you, G-George. P-put theshe c-cuffsh on G-George,

Even if he ish on the sc-shcool board." Since Charley
Was out, he and my father and the officers
Lifted the Model T by the bumpers,
While my mother drove a little down the road
And parked beside a mooing Holstein herd,
Their heads over the fence rail, slowly chewing.
My father came walking along the sand,
Calm as Pike's Peak, felt of some dents and scratches,
And said, "A little more work for the Biezk Boys."
A scent of cowpies filled the Sabbath air.

Grayland Apocalypse

In the year the United States landed on the moon,
I stood at the Pacific edge, near Grayland,
Watching the breakers toss a blue ghost-mist:
It was October, and my wife and daughter
Were far down-beach searching for sand dollars,
So I went and sat on a driftwood Douglas fir
Near a faded Russian crate, and thought of my joy
Despite the national crisis. In a happy trance,
I was somewhat surprised to see twelve angels
Wandering toward me along the tideline.

The first shuffled and swayed like a Kodiak bear
And carried a rose; it was certainly Ted Roethke.
Beside him William Blake danced through the surf,
Walt Whitman sauntered, chewing a stalk of sedge,
And Edward Lear, wearing a runcible hat,
Accompanied by his rotund cat, Old Foss,
Carried a large sieve with a pea-green sail.
Seagulls shrieked, drifted and wheeled above them
And a line of sandpipers ran near their images,
Where razor clam shells spread wing in the draining waves.

Following at some distance was Nathaniel Hawthorne,
His sorrowful face lit by an inward joy:
I remembered reading his stories at seven,
Curled in the old leather chair at Elm.
At his side was ambling William Wordsworth,
In brown fustian jacket and striped pantaloons.
Both were deep in contemplation, but often
Laughed at a remark by E. E. Cummings,
Who wore a beret and a pre-Raphaelite necktie,
Or Vachel Lindsay, with a 1910 auto horn

Borrowed from his poem, "The Santa Fe Trail."
The last four were led by Countee Cullen

In bush cut and bright African attire,
Wearing a small crucifix on a necklace,
And William Langland in a shepherd's habit.
Behind them, side by side on the hard-packed sand,
Came Robert Frost, holding a piece of birch bark,
And T. S. Eliot carrying the Holy Grail.
Each of the twelve appeared to have six wings,
But Old Foss was sporting only four.

Roethke said, "Hello, Moose, you've been chosen."
"What for, Ted?" I asked. "To go to Michigan
For a short vision," he said and pulled from his pocket
Some Bible leaves, rolled and tied with green ribbon,
"You'd better eat this, first." "O.K. What is it?"
"The Book of Ezekiel," he said with a kind of shrug.
"I hope to God it's the Revised Standard Version,"
I said. "For Christ's sake," he said kicking a clam
Shell, "Would I ask you to swallow the King James?
You might choke on a mistranslated metaphor."

"How are we going to get there?" I enquired,
"I remember how Ezekiel got around
From Babylon to Jerusalem." "Lucky you've still
Got your hair." "It's a long way to Michigan,"
I said. "Yeah. Actually we've fixed up something else."
I looked askance at Edward Lear's large sieve.
"Moose, what do you see just over that dune?"
"I see, behold, the ghost of Uncle Wiggily,
My 1950 Chevrolet." "Yeah," said Ted,
"It stopped running the same month I did.

We repaired it in an old Goodyear plant.
Look at the tires." "I notice it has eyes
All the way around the 4 wheels,
Seven headlamps, and an olive tree for aerial."
"You and I'll ride in front," said Ted,
"Robert, Estlin and Vachel in the back seat,

And the others will fly, two beside each wheel."
Then he cast a wry gaze at Old Foss
And said, I'll take this fleabag on my lap."
"Just a minute, Ted. Why was I chosen?"

"Remember your birthday in 1956,
How we played bocce under the horse chestnuts?
And we talked about Herbert, Vaughan, and Thomas,
And I gave you my last first edition of *The Lost Son*?
Haven't you taught the Bible As Literature 12 years?
Weren't you baptized in water from the Jordan?
Didn't your parents pray for you all one night
Of childhood illness? Don't you know Auden backwards?
I told Old Dad you were the man. Come on,
Eat your Ezekiel and let's get going."

"How was this little delegation of angels picked?"
"We represent your major influences."
With this Ted handed me a bottle of Guinness Stout,
To wash Ezekiel down. It took ten minutes
And tasted bitter, but once down, felt like honey.
We climbed into Uncle Wiggily and took off,
Our backs to the sun. Crossing the Cascades,
I steered toward Cripple Creek, to show Ted
The place of my mother's childhood, which I once
Visited at 22. Lindsay leaned out the window

Honking his horn and reciting, "The Santa Fe Trail"
And Ted played jazz on the car's radio,
Which received FM through the olive tree.
"As God is my witness," said Ted above the Rockies,
"I was going to write about all this, like Walt."
He looked at Whitman who moved in easy flaps
Like a seagull on a gale, near the left front wheel.
"Look at that. I loaf, and invite my soul,"
Said Ted, giving Cummings a sniff of his rose.
"Well, Nelson, let's head toward Detroit."

As Uncle Wiggily floated over Michigan
I could see all the way to Saginaw,
At the base of the thumb, and thought of Father
Marquette's remark on muskrats. I steered
Instinctively toward a classical stone building
Looming through smog near downtown Detroit.
"Land on the front steps," said Roethke.
We and the 8 angels simultaneously alit.
"What do you see, Moose?" "I see, behold,
The Detroit Public Library. Why are we here?"

"This is where you found the American poets
You couldn't find anyplace else," said Ted.
"What was that main street we flew along,
Moose?" "Grand River. When my father was a boy
He drove downtown with vegetables on Grand River,
In a wagon hitched to his horse, Old Maud,
Named from Tennyson, past onion farms
Now full of skyscrapers. At 14, I drove
Our International egg truck, Bosco, the same road.
On the tailgate it said, "We have been laying for you."

We all got out, and Ted and I climbed up
On Uncle Wiggily's roof, by the olive tree.
The other eleven angels and Old Foss
Formed a circle around the car and danced
To the music and words of Edward Lear's "The Jumblies,"
As Cummings used Lear's sieve for a tambourine.
I was surprised at the gaiety and joyful leaps
Of Hawthorne and T. S. Eliot; Wordsworth almost
Fell down laughing, but was quickly steadied
By Vachel Lindsay and Old Foss. Curious students

Were gathering, as Roethke pointed west and said,
"What do you see, Moose?" "I see a jet plane,
Flying above Grand River. On second thought,
It looks like a 1970 Plymouth, and is pouring out

A thick multicolored cloud of smoke
Settling all over the city." "You know what the smoke
Is, of course?" asked Ted. "What is it?" I replied.
"That is the Profit Motive, also called Mammon."
The Plymouth now hovered above J. L. Hudson's,
Where I had my hair cut while riding a zebra, at six.

The smoke hung over the city like an awful halo.
Roethke said, "America must choose.
Emerson and Thoreau saw her opposite aims.
The Profit Motive will be subordinated
To the love of God and neighbor, or the nation
Falls. Remember in my film, 'poetry says
You must change your life.' I knew that long
Ago in Saginaw, and you, Hayden and Brinnin
In Detroit. The place to decide is here and now:
Immediately, as all the gospels say."

I took a firm grasp of the olive tree,
And watched 8 of the angels fly toward the Plymouth.
They removed the hubcaps and held them carefully
High above Detroit. "What are they doing?" I asked.
"They will empty 4 hubcaps full of the Wrath of God,
Or the consequences of America's sins.
The first hubcap is filled with nationalism."
Then Balek and Lindsay dumped the first hubcap,
And napalm burst aflame in Cadillac Square
From a container covered with stars and stripes.

At this point I fainted flat on the radiator,
With one arm flung backward across a headlight.
I awoke, as Roethke was emptying a six-pack
Of Budweiser on my face and fanning his wings.
"Come on, Moose, for the love of God. They're dumping
The second hubcap." I staggered to my feet
As Walt Whitman and Countee Cullen overturned
The hubcap of racism high over the ghettoes

And a great light revealed the poor and sick,
Suppressed and unemployed and isolated.

The Plymouth backfired, and a denser smoke
Poured from the exhaust, from which emerged
E. E. Cummings and Nathaniel Hawthorne,
With the third hubcap. They poured it where I thought
The Fox Theater stood. A multicolored
Chemical fell, deranging all it touched.
"What is that?" I asked. Roethke replied,
"That is the hubcap of sensuality.
It replaces love with lust, decays the soul,
Commercializes the sense, and makes bad art."

I sank to my knees and watched as William Langland
And Edward Lear rather informally dumped
The last hubcap over the Detroit River:
"This is the hubcap of indifference,"
Said Roethke, as pouring chemicals polluted
The air and waters, several stage curtains fell
Concealing the ghettoes, and the radio announced
A new moon landing. This time I fainted
Crosswise on the radiator like an old horse blanket
We used on our Marmon at zero in the depression.

Roused by Roethke's last Budweiser, I slid
To the Library steps and zigzagged slowly up
To where T. S. Eliot stood beside two egg crates,
One on either side of the main entrance.
He wore a look of kindly concern. Old Foss
Stood on his shoulder. "Nelson, what do you see?"
Asked Eliot. "Eggs," I said. My boyhood days
Of egg-candling came back in a flash.
"One crate of very good eggs. Fresh, A-1,"
I said; "the other appears mainly rotten.

The smell is evident; the shells are desiccated,
Sort of gray or green, rather like the moon
When Armstrong stepped on it. I would guess
The insides are shrunken, several have dead
Embryo chicks and watery or bloody spots.
They may have been found in old nests under the henhouse."
"These good eggs," said Eliot, "are the Americans
Who confess their country's sins, nationalism,
Racism, lust, indifference and the Profit Motive,
And who turn again to sacrificial love.

The bad eggs are the complacent, with closed minds,
Decaying in their egos. Or, as I put it earlier,
Our choice is the Waste Land or the Rose Garden.
God's Wrath is always exceeded by His Mercy."
Then I heard a great chorus of cries,
And saw the starving children of the world
On the roof of the Detroit Public Library,
Watching United States bombers and moon rockets
Cross overhead; the sky grew dark as dusk
And I looked around, expecting maybe a whirlwind.

What I saw, though, was only E.E. Cummings,
Countee Cullen, Frost, and Roethke, kneeling
As though caught in a visionary rapture
Near the bottom of the steps, gazing toward
The Detroit River. Cullen beckoned, and I went
To kneel beside him and follow his upward look.
Then I saw Jesus, standing on the smog
Above Belle Isle, where I picnicked as a child;
His right hand was reaching toward the Library,
And his head was in a radiance like sunrise.

"He is the Way and the Good News," said Cummings.
"He is the Bread of Life, called Wonderful.
He builds strong minds twelve different ways."
"Is this the Second Coming?" I enquired.

"The Second Coming is in the individual,"
Said Frost, "When He is manifest in your choice
Of action. I found that out at Kitty Hawk."
Then a river of light streamed from the Library doors,
Down the stairs to Woodward Avenue,
And fanned out in four directions through Detroit.

Everywhere the river went, people were filled
With joy and dancing, inward healing, selfless love
And individual difference. I noticed Cullen
And Roethke doing a joyful African dance
Up Woodward, along one branch of the river,
Followed by Cummings, Hawthorne, Lindsay and Langland,
A multitude of the poor and hungry, and every
Ethnic minority of the city. Then I saw standing
Back where the river started, Wordsworth and Blake;
I climbed the stairs and asked, "What is this river?"

"It is spiritual Love," Wordsworth answered;
"This spiritual Love acts not nor can exist
Without Imagination. See *The Prelude*,
Book 14." Then Blake added, "The last judgment
Is not fable or allegory but vision. All things
Are comprehended in their eternal forms
In the divine body of the Saviour, the true vine
Of eternity, the human imagination."
I then danced on the Library steps with Frost,
Whitman, Lear, Eliot and Old Foss

Until Roethke returned, lumbering through
An intricate jazz step, swinging a tennis racket.
"Well, Moose, let's get back in Uncle Wiggily,"
He said. "Can you put this in a poem? Remember,
You've got the Word of God in you, washed down
With Guinness Stout." "I'll try, Ted. I swear
By Edward Taylor and the Far Field full of light."
All the way to Grayland we sang Irish ballads

And Lear's Complete Nonsense, and soon were dipping
Down toward the blue breakers of the Pacific coast.

I could see all the monoliths and headlands
From LaPush to Cannon Beach. Roethke said,
"Take it easy, Moose. We'll drop you by the driftwood."
So I stepped out, three feet above a dune,
And watched Uncle Wiggily soar north toward Westport,
By the ever fresh, endless thunder of the surf.
I walked to the tideline through starred sandpiper prints
And looked across seven lines of breaking waves.
Then Beth and Julian came running through their reflections,
Their hands full of sand dollars without price.

December 1969

The Ozette Trail

Through cedar and hemlock in dry August
In America's forest furthest west,
I walked old truncheon planks of spruce,
Rocks, earth, needles, ancient roots,
Four miles of trail, and up the coast
In pilgrimage to the Ozette past,
To get a good look at the present,
A reactionary president,
The worship of money and napalm,
Opposites of what we started from.

I climbed from my old red Chevrolet
In the year of Our Lord 1970
And stood by Ozette in the wilderness
Like Deerslayer by the Glimmerglass,
Emerson by the Concord, or Thoreau,
Remembering a red cedar canoe,
High prow painted with a bear's head,
Then started into the forest, led
By Sean, with the back-pack, at 16,
And my nine-year daughter, Julian.

Beth walked last, all through the hike-in,
Identifying leaves and lichen.
Ozette ghosts filled the air; the odor
Of moss hung lightly in the alder
Whose gray and white trunks once made cradles,
Salmon-smoke wood and canoe paddles,
And hemlock whose cooked juice painted masks
For dancing, and sealed the water-baskets;
Squirrels and woodpeckers called
Through green air that seemed ocean-filled.

Around us fragrant red cedar
Grew canoes for whaling and war,

Or potlatch bowls, or plank homes
By Cape Alava's stormy foams.
Salal, whose berries, mashed and dried,
Dipped in whale oil, were baked on a board,
The pure, cold, tannin-colored streams,
The Indian cough-medicine, licorice ferns,
And salmonberry, browsed by elk,
Held the past, as though to calk.

Nearer the ocean, Sitka spruce
Grew thick in coast winds cool and moist,
Great trunks purple-brown and scaled,
Papery cones all along the trail:
Their roots made baskets and rain hats,
Their pitch protected harpoon points
When canoes pursued gray whale and seal
For the Ozette village food and oil,
And whale bones built a deeper midden
For archaeologists to dig in.

Scattered in spruce, Douglas firs
Plunged higher in the atmosphere,
A hundred feet before a branch:
Light fell from them like an avalanche,
To be absorbed by weeping hemlocks,
Deer fern and mossed, decaying logs.
I remembered the double row of pines
Still as light on the Rocky Mountains,
When we took my mother to her grave
In Plymouth, when I was twenty-five:

This zigzag ceremonial trail,
Like that last ride up gravel,
Awakened the detail of regrets,
Like rediscovering the Ozettes
Whose artifacts lie in solution
Beside the unchanging ocean.

I remembered Elm Woods where, a child,
I entered the realm of the wild
And learned from red squirrel, crow and rabbit,
Garter snake, frog, and jack-in-the-pulpit:

And thought of Black Lake's parchment birch,
Like pages waiting for new verse.
While the spruce planks led me on,
Our footsteps' incantation
Fell into fours as the trail veered,
And became the voices of poets. I heard
Pondering their times in this meter
Shelley, Auden, Arnold, Whittier,
Evoking mankind's goods and ills
From New York to the Euganean Hills.

Stepping on planks of cedar and spruce,
Past downed logs covered with thick moss
And lichen, stumps turned garden,
Dense shade which the alders brighten,
Hemlock and spruce in colonnade
From humus of logs long decayed,
Roots straddling moldered trunks,
Vine maples' green translucence,
Swollen, fluted trunks of cedars,
Silver firs, resin-blistered,

I walked those luminous green miles,
Tree frog and woodpecker-sung aisles
Between the deep-ridged Douglas fir,
Sounds of ocean in my ear:
From a stair of cedar trunk, cross-sawn,
The trail dropped softly down a dune
To a beach of drift logs and black gravel,
The old Ozette home, Capa Alava,
A place to clarify belief,
Guarded by islands, rocks and reef.

Monoliths covered with seabird lime,
Seal homes, spray-washed as long as time,
The Flattery Rocks wildlife refuge
Clear to the Umatilla Reef,
Indian Island, a sea stack
Forest-topped, the gravelly squawk
Of gulls that by the hundreds float
A slow salt wind, told the Ozette
Way of the hand-hewn whale canoe
Which ended seventy years ago.

North up the coast, wading streams,
Through gulls' and pipers' shrills and screams,
Past great logs thrown by winter storms
Beyond the high tide's usual norms,
We walked the brown sea wrack and sand,
Each wave pushing shells up land,
And, showing some signs of fatigue,
Reached the archaeological dig.
In chemical solution lay
The Ozette history, tray by tray,

Washed from earth by pressure hoses:
Baskets like the one of Moses,
Wooden harpoon shafts, rainhats, combs,
Floormats, arrows, mixing bowls,
Preserved by mudslides from 1900
Back to millenia unnumbered;
And, carved with detailed artist's love,
Three flawless, black, seal-shaped seal-clubs,
Ears, eyes, flippers, whiskers, nostrils,
Reverent for the required kills.

Then, the archaeologists' prize,
Found yesterday by modern eyes,
Half out of mud, a potlatch bowl
The size of a small whaling boat,

Full of curved designs of teeth
From otter, whale and seal. The wealth
Was once distributed by gift,
In Chinook, potlatch: time will sift
Our values, actual and mythic,
Like this dig by the Pacific.

The tribe, a branch of the Makahs,
Perished from our disease and laws,
The remnant scattered in their nation
By compulsory education.
The dig was drawing near the bounds
Of its small federal funds,
Ended as it had just begun
By America's new war machine:
Would our next hike find Ozette forms
Taken out to sea by storms?

I tried to gaze like the Ozettes
At ten thousand years of sunsets
Beyond the looming basalt stacks,
Tossed lines of surf, harbor seals' barks,
Whales migrating spring and fall,
Gulls' constant cries, antiphonal,
Kelp beds with vanished sea otters
Whose pelts removed them from these waters,
And thought of petroglyphs in basalt
A mile down coast, at Wedding Rock

Where, outside time, carved men and whales
Dance in dark Ozette haloes;
On the Columbia, near Vantage,
Such art is now safe from damage,
Sunk deep by the Wanapum Dam.
Some chunks cut loose for a museum
Show man and wife, children and deer,
Heads crowned by sunray and antler,

Their air of serenity and peace
Arranged beside a precipice,

From which they gaze toward Wanapum
A mile downstream. The turbines' hum
Encloses another museum
Where salmon-window viewers come,
And, for a moment, may grow humble
Before an earlier Columbia:
Implements, baskets and costumes,
Above the dam in four small rooms,
And words ecologists will hallow,
A prophecy of Smohalla.

I thought of small bright arrowheads,
Chipped especially to kill birds
Or fish, on those Columbia islands
Which lakes have covered behind dams,
Lost rapids with their salmon spears
Sacrificed to volts and gears,
Invisible villages and canoes,
Drowned islands of the Memaloose.
Once in the dam at Rocky Beach, a
Little upriver from Wenatchee,

Our guide was a descendant of
Chiefs Moses and Young Joseph,
Dressed in buckskin, tooth and shell,
Bead and feather. She could tell
The story back of every mural
As we walked above the waters' whirl
And looked out at the stream of cars
Racing along asphalt curves.
Thinking of power and love, I
Started back from Cape Alava.

Downcoast by barnacle-white rocks,
Bright air saturate with squawks,
Great barkless stumps washed in by seas
Ramming the beaches, Portuguese
Men-of-war (blue jellyfish
Topped with sails), anemones
And sea urchins in each tidepool,
Starfish stuck to rocks like glue,
We stopped at a horizontal fir
To roast hot dogs by a driftwood fire.

Out in the shallows, a blue heron
Suggested how we ought to listen,
Then, like an incarnated myth,
Went flapping past a monolith.
I imagined the Ozettes, ancient and safe,
Netting smelt in the spring surf,
Living on salmon, clams and mussels,
Berries, roots, elk, deer, and whales.
I sat dreaming in the salty smoke
Of a presence the past must evoke.

Once, in drift logs near LaPush,
Listening to surf and spruce,
We spent four nights under canvas
And walked through morning's thinning mist
To Hole-In-The-Wall, a granite shoulder
Through which the ocean had worn a door:
Offshore stood the Quillayute Needles.
I saw a metaphor from the gospels,
And knowing the choice is love or death,
Walked, through the eye of the Needles, north.

Our driftwood fire was down to coals.
The sun fell toward seastacks and shoals
And lit the winging, wave-slow dance

By rock of gulls and cormorants.
In the cupped hands of Julian, we
Saw hermit crabs with red antennae
Held with love's curious delight;
It was time to go. The Ozette night
In three hours would completely fill
The woods. We started up the trail.

September 1970

Iron Man of the Hoh

A mile at sea, Cake Rock, against the blue,
Lifts its seafowl sanctuary. Harsh squawks
    Float from the monoliths. A few
High breakers begin their crests and churns,
As I watch the sun sinking toward sea stacks,
            And the world turns.

Again I've walked this tideline near La Push
From the Quillayute River to Hole In The Wall.
    Offshore the rocks, like gods, stand fresh,
Unshaken by all the ocean's worst in storms,
Their only voice in cormorant and gull:
            And the world turns.

A dozen times I've walked it with Applebaum,
Painter and raconteur. One time he told
    Me, with his monolithic aplomb,
As we strode along on shells and fish skeletons,
The story of the Iron Man of the Hoh:
            And the world turns

On such accounts. It seems this Northwest Samson
Carried an iron cookstove twenty miles
    Up the Hoh on his back, having
Homesteaded among Douglas firs, moss and ferns
In 1890. And as God made little apples,
            And the world turns,

Two loggers, who saw him trotting the stove through the wood,
Asked, "Isn't that heavy? " He said, "No, but it's hard
    To keep my balance on a log
When the sack of flour shifts in the oven."
So he raised his family far from any road;
            And the world turns.

This man, John Huelsdonk, killed 300 cougars,
Once had his leg lacerated by a bear,
    Crawled home 2 miles through firs and cedars,
And then walked 40 miles into Forks.
His daughter pulled two men out of the Hoh by their hair;
        And the world turns.

My wife and daughter, at the tidal edge,
Move by Cake Rock, which now, against the sun,
    Goes purple-brown with the light's change,
Their pockets full of agates and odd stones.
My campfire gives the wind a pungent stain.
        And the world turns.

Well, I've seen Babe Ruth hit two home runs
At Navin Field, Frost at 75,
    Auden juggling the concerns
Of his century, Thomas in two taverns,
And Roethke, one of the giants of the alive;
        And the world turns

Into legend. I remember Jean Garrigue
Embracing a Douglas fir in the Rain Forest.
    Applebaum has fished among
Those basalt giants on which the seagull mourns.
Is that you, John Huelsdonk, where the breakers start?
        And the world turns

Purple-blue in dusk. I think of how
My parents loved, imagined, and endured.
    I gather wood and watch gulls float
On gathering breakers and settle on the crags.
The sun enters the ocean, a ball of blood,
        And the world turns.

September 1971

Green Lake Apocalypse

1.
At dawn after the Republican convention
I woke to a hundred swallows on the light wires
Criticizing a whippoorwill's intention,
As he slept with a look like J. Edgar Hoover's
On a rusty T.V. antenna. One recovers
Slowly when soused with Goldwatered Sousa,
So I drove two miles to Green Lake, giving the Muse a

Chance, and started walking the bicycle path
By willows and cedars, thinking of Thoreau,
Nixon's nationalism and God's Wrath.
Along came a man with a wheelbarrow
Containing fig baskets, red, white and blue.
He wore a loincloth and a Sasquatch wig,
And remarked, clearly, "Nixon's a bad fig."

"Holy Jerusalem," I said, "you're Jeremiah."
"Nelson," he answered, "who's coming down the lane?"
"Walt Whitman, with a carpenter's level and straw
Hat," I said, "Amos, carrying a plumb line;
Oh-oh, Herman Melville, with a bent harpoon;
And Isaiah, I think, dressed only in a bumper
Strip, which—just a minute—reads 'Make love, not war'."

"He's worn that during two administrations,
Riding bumpers throughout the United States.
Next comes the Parade Between Two Oceans,
Which we've arranged with some unusual floats.
It's led by a phalanx of five thousand fat cats,
Who live on unction-flavored gasoline.
By the way," he said, "I heard last Hallowe'en

You dressed as me." "I hope that was O.K.
Herman Melville was there, and Dylan Thomas

And Fern Hill." As the cats were passing by,
I saw float low an angel with a bulbous
Red nose and six wings, four of which held bottles;
With two, he flew. As he settled slowly down,
I noticed his glowing cigar and bright nightgown.

"Come one, come all," said Fields, tipping his hat
To Jeremiah. "On all this continent,
Your eyes will not observe a stranger beast.
Behold the wonderful 4-headed elephant,
Who will perform an inimitable stunt."
The 4 heads made me wish for a cathartic:
Goldwater, Reagan, Agnew, Joe McCarthy.

John Wayne was swaggering ten yards in front,
In a buckskin suit hand-sewn by Whistler's Mother,
And carried six flags; atop the elephant
Sat Richard Nixon, dressed like Cotton Mather,
Beneath an umbrella shaped like a bomber.
He carried a cross combined with a dollar sign,
The words "Perfectly clear" on the horizontal line.

Around his head circled a winged football,
Its seven eyes fixed steadily on Nixon.
Then Fields remarked, wings juggling a bottle,
"This elephant's rider is the only American,
So far as is known, to have seen the movie *Patton*
Forty-two times. On the elephant's legs, by the way,
Are strapped the complete works of Zane Grey.

The creature is the son of Wide Awake,
Sleepiest elephant on the entire globe."
Then each of the four heads raised a wrinkled trunk
And bellowed like Saul at the priests of Nob,
"Pusillanimous pussyfooters!" "Shades of Job,"
Said Fields, flinching and glancing toward the sky,
"The elephant trumpets: who can but prophesy?"

2.
Next came ambling along, a humble ass,
With Humpty-Dumpty riding on his rear;
The ass chewed thoughtfully upon a rose,
While Lyndon Johnson tugged at him and swore,
Under a ten-gallon hat reading "War galore."
Between curses Johnson wore a look of piety,
And waved a rag that said "The Great Society."

Across Green Lake then flew, on six large wings,
With a sound not unlike Niagara's roar,
An angel, brighter than fifty Mobilgas signs,
Who had four heads like those on Mt. Rushmore
And carried George McGovern by the hair.
Seeing the angel, the ass turned aside.
Johnson kicked him, saying "Cuss yo' shaggy hide,

Git back thar on the right-of-way." The angel
Stood on the path between two madrona trees.
The ass backed away, all meek and gentle,
And hitting a tree, bruised one of Humpty's knees.
Johnson kicked him, saying, "Cuss yo' shaggy hide,
Ah am yo' lord and master. Have yo' no awe?"
The ass succinctly answered, "Hee haw."

The angel looked simultaneously south,
North, east and west, and stood upon a bridge;
The ass lay down in the middle of the path,
Spilling Humpty-Dumpty on one edge,
With forty cracks under his Democratic badge.
Johnson kicked the ass with fury and abandon;
The Lord opened the mouth of the ass, who said to Lyndon:

"What have I done to you, that you have kicked
Me these 3 times?" Johnson narrowed his eyes
And said, "Yo' have made sport of me, and bucked
Mah authority. Ah might just surprise

Yo' with mah six-shootah, and cut yo' down to size."
The sky was suddenly lit by more than gas.
The ass said, "Am I not your faithful ass,

Upon which you have ridden these forty years?"
Seven lightning bolts showed a change of weather.
Then Johnson picked the ass up by his ears,
And said, "Come now, let us reason togethah."
The ass said, "Isaiah one, but finish the chapter."
Then Fields remarked, "Glory, hallelujah.
The mountain has flown in from South Dakota."

The angel flung McGovern on the saddle;
The ass galloped off like lightning. Fields called,
"I hope you make that elephant skedaddle."
Then Amos, Whitman and Jeremiah strolled
Up with Isaiah and Melville, the Greek Lake Fold.
Fields opened an Old Crow, took seven swallows,
Then the five prophets, Fields, and I spoke as follows:

3.

Whitman:

Nelson, the week we met at Paumanok
When you were twenty, long before the pattern
Of America turned over Plymouth Rock,
We saw the nation's aims like George McGovern;
But Nixon throws his prophets in the cistern,
And announces he is zagging when he zigs.

Chorus:

America, don't swallow those bad figs.

Amos:

For three imperialist transgressions, and for four,
Says the Lord, I will smite Key Biscayne.
The elephant trumpets of aerial war.
Seek the Lord and live, lest a Hurricane
Burst like napalm on the house of Nixon.
Nationalism is waving all its flags.

Chorus:

America, don't swallow those bad figs.

Fields:

Whitman, thou shouldst be living at this hour.
But since you're not, Bentley will have to do.
Our problem is Nixon, son of Eisenhower,
Rider of the purple sage, and his friend Agnew.
In the worst national crisis since '32
Their answers are what Maggie does to Jiggs.

Chorus:

America, don't swallow those bad figs.

Isaiah:

Nelson, think of Ezekiel by the Chebar,
Wordsworth by the Wye, Arnold in Kensington Gardens,
Daniel by the Tigris, Watkins in Gower,
John on Patmos, Moody by Lake Michigan,
Thoreau's majority of one at Walden:

Their selfless love baffled the bigwigs.
Chorus:
America, don't swallow those bad figs.

Melville:
Nixon and Jonah say "Smash Nineveh;"
Jonah to make himself a famous prophet,
Nixon to make "respect for the presidency."
Their expressions resemble that of Claggart,
Or Ahab with the white whale as a target;
The whale, swallowing either of them, gags.
Chorus:
America, don't swallow those bad figs.

Jeremiah:
I've been against Richard Nixon all along,
Since the day he told a Babylonian
"Nothing my nation ever does is wrong."
You elected him for his Secret Plan
Which was, to become a flying Genghis Khan.
His beliefs are static as whirligigs.
Chorus:
America, don't swallow those bad figs.

Bentley:
From Paumanok, I climbed into Liberty's forehead;
Mother of Exiles, our genocidal turn
Lay in the future. This is the watershed;
Will we confess our sins through George McGovern,
And the vision of Emma Lazarus be reborn?
Will we be more than archaeological digs?
Chorus:
America, don't swallow those bad figs.

August-September 1972

Jeremiah's Words at Christmas For Nixon's Second Inauguration

In the beginning, the U.S. first
Read Genesis around the moon;
A week before the birth of Christ
Moonship *America* splashed down
And Nixon's bombers went to town.
The pseudo-Quaker doffed his wigs
With record raids where skins are brown.
It's four more years of naughty figs.

Whitman and Whittier watch aghast;
Ben Franklin's hair is straight on end;
Nixon, the new Galloping Ghost,
Zigzags toward the Torrid Zone.
Vultures amble the White House lawn,
Newsmen are ready for the brigs,
And God is acted by John Wayne:
It's four more years of naughty figs.

I'm thinking of the potter's flask,
Almond rod, new covenant:
Remember Kennedy and Frost?
Now we'll have Nixon's T.V. frown,
Like Grendel's from his gloomy fen:
America's unself, with flags,
Antithesis of John Woolman.
It's four more years of naughty figs.

King Richard, in your four year reign,
Know, while you hobnob with the bigs,
My loincloth molds on Key Biscayne;
It's four more years of naughty figs.

December, 1972

Coeur d'Alene Apocalypse

1.
In the first April of Nixon's second term,
I had paused on the way to Idaho
By Indian petroglyphs on the Columbia,
Where men and gods are mingled on the stone:
An angel, than which I'd seen none clumsier,
          Flew like a shell-shocked worm
Down the gorge, calling, "Get your *Day of Doom*,
Light summer reading." His stern face stared forth;
His forty-two bat wings cast an eerie gloom.
"Good Lord!" I said. "It's Michael Wigglesworth."

Behind him flew an enormous angel,
Bellowing, "O lost and by the wind grieved ghost,
Come back again." His eyes, like those of Coleridge
In "Kubla Khan," wildly flashed and tossed.
He beat his head on the bumper of a carriage,
          His black hair in a tangle
Over the bumper strip, which read, "Congress
Is constitutionally inappropriate."
The carriage, I saw, was the most incongruous
Checker Cab in the United States.

On its roof stood Richard Nixon, dressed and posed
Like George Washington crossing the Delaware,
Two checkers resting regally on his head.
Inside, Haldeman, Ehrlichman and Ziegler
Scowled like Rachmaninoff, or dyspeptic bloodhounds.
          A sign on the windshield
Read "Inoperative." Behind flew, looking sick,
John Greenleaf Whittier, a clothespin on his nose,
Playing a record of Handel's "Water Music."
Above soared a bird, half eagle and half crow,

Crying, "Woe, woe, woe to the Four Gates that led
King Richard to the White House: the Fire Gate,
The Air Gate, the Earth Gate, and the Water
Gate." As if in answer, a sky rocket
Came from the cab's exhaust pipe, with a sputter.
The bird clutched a deflated
Football in its talons, and a Quaker Oats
Box hung on its neck, as on a Saint Bernard's.
The eagle-crow and Nixon cleared their throats
And spoke, or croaked, in unison these words:

"April is the cruellest month. This music
Crept by me upon the waters." Nixon added,
"Kennedy quoted Eliot: so can I."
The corners of his mouth gradually sagged
Like a putrescent jack o' lantern. Then the sky
Turned somewhat pale and phthisic
As Thomas Wolfe yelled, "Look homeward, angel!"
And Nixon said, "My feet are at Watergate.
Drip drop drip drop drop drop drop." His lapel,
I saw, held a pin saying, "Remember Zane Grey."

Suddenly, 3-1/2 flagpoles popped up
From the cab's roof, flapping with Old Glory,
The bloodhounds put on six large round black ears,
And, while Nixon's eyelashes fluttered madly,
This song came from the cab full of Zieglers:
"Who's the leader of the club,
Who's All-American? R--I--C,
K--E--Y, N--I--X--O--N."
Then a red streamer unfurled endlessly,
Labelled, "Enemies of the administration."

With a look of sanctimonious disdain,
Nixon folded the flags into his burglar kit
The size of an orange crate, with gold embossed
Words: "After all, I am the President."
Wolfe, Wigglesworth and Whittier cried, "Follow us
Nelson, to Coeur d'Alene."
I leaped in my Chevrolet and sped through sage
Along I-90, my eye on the Checker Cab,
Red streamer, and 3 angels, Wolfe's words of rage
Bouncing toward me like the tumbleweed.

2.
Above Lake Coeur d'Alene, a green helicopter
Hovered beside a steep, forested shore
Near the Green Dolphin Restaurant. I saw
An angel with lantern nose float from the door,
Holding a Bible and a bottle of Old Crow.
            He was reading a chapter
From the *Collected Poems of William Blake*,
And rasping the words of "Bringing in the Sheaves."
He dropped like an old elevator toward the lake.
I noticed, issuing from Blake's and the Bible's leaves,

Two angels: Jonah, with a huge placard
Reading "Bomb Nineveh," and Oothoon,
The soul of America. The Checker Cab,
Skyrockets firing from all sides of Nixon,
Bristled with binoculars; a loud tape
            Repeated, "Nixon wrong? Never."
Fields extended me his hand, with a bottle of beer,
And said, "Fear not! I come from Golgonooza,
In order to make one thing perfectly clear:
When Nixon makes a mistake, it's a lalapalooza."

He added, juggling his books and bottle,
"You observed the bit of prestidigitation
Producing Jonah, here, and Oothoon?
This signifies the choice before the nation:
If memory serves, yonder Richard Nixon
            Was coughed up by a whale
Five years ago. May I suggest a stroll,
A mile up Mineral Ridge, to Caribou Cabin?
Where we'll prepare, for that presidential foul ball,
An all-star vision, featuring Walt Whitman."

Fields and I climbed through ponderosa pine,
A hundred birdsongs floating past mossy trunks.
He sang and whistled "The Old Oaken Bucket,"

Pausing every few bars for a couple of drinks:
Then "Moon Over Miami," "A Tisket, A Tasket,"
          "The Wearing Of The Green,"
And "A Dicky-bird sat on the limb of a tree,
Singing Willow, tit-willow, tit-willow."
He then remarked, rather off-handedly,
"Have you noticed, Nixon looks like an armadillo?"

At Caribou Cabin, above Lake Coeur d'Alene,
Walt Whitman sat, eating milk and biscuits.
"Heavens to Betsy, you're poisoning yourself,"
Said Fields. The sound of two colonial muskets,
In Nixon's hands, came from the Checker Cab's roof,
          Which now held a large sign,
"200th Anniversary coming soon."
Fields said, "Walt, where did Nixon first go wrong?"
"He never read *Passage To India*," said Whitman.
The pines seemed filled to brimming with birdsong.

Walt walked from the cabin and called "Camerados!"
A wind like surf surged through the ponderosas.
All past American poets from Anne Bradstreet
To Jean Garrigue, from Taylor to William Carlos
Williams, from Freneau to Theodore Roethke,
          Floated from the pine woods
And formed a circle around the Checker Cab,
Began a ceremonial war dance, and shot
A thousand quotations at Nixon. "You're all a fib,"
He said, scowling. "And I might add, Poppycock!"

Then I saw Fields and Whitman near the headlights,
Above Beauty Bay, near Poet's Point;
Fields called, "Read Nehemiah 8 and Matthew 7;
Discover why your nose is out of joint."
Walt bellowed like an elk, "I am Walt Whitman,
          A kosmos. Unscrew the locks
From the doors! Unscrew the doors from their jambs!"

Nixon's mouth turned down like the Wizard of Oz,
And his cab's 4 tires blew out with mighty blams.
I fainted, flat as a run-over fox,

Beside Caribou Cabin. I woke as Fields
Poured Budweiser on my face. "Great somersaulting
Snakes," he said. "You just missed Nixon's rescue
By the Goodyear Blimp." I watched the blimp go wafting
Toward Key Biscayne, blinking these words in blue:
            "3-1/2 more years."
Then Fields and I wove down past Silver Tip,
Singing, "Did your mother come from Ireland?"
Toward the Green Dolphin for a little sip,
Through the ponderosas and a freshening wind.

July 1973

Uncle Clyde at Armageddon

"For I believe the spiritual combat to be more desperate
in the center of chaos, which is Detroit."
—Theodore Roethke, in STRAW FOR THE FIRE

Canto 1.
What in Sam Hill can I say, American Muse,
To invoke your aid in capturing Uncle Clyde?
Remember the day I pondered in your forehead,
In New York Bay, looking toward the Atlantic,
The shade of Whitman standing at my side,
Fresh from Paumanok, where I, like Walt,
Spent a day reciting Shakespeare to the seagulls?
It was in the decade I emerged from childhood,
In the Depression, which seems to have swirled
Around that mighty lighthouse, the Old Dutch Mill.

Muse of Mark Twain and W. C. Fields,
Of Thurber, Buster Keaton, Roethke and Harpo,
Look upon Five Mile Road and Middlebelt
Where Clyde's 500 flags, tattered and dim,
Were stuck between the fan-shaped signs that read,
"Our eggs are so fresh they shouldn't be sold
Until tomorrow," "Eggs laid while you wait,"
and "Chickens dressed and undressed." And call back
The days of Barney Google, Andy Gump,
Mutt and Jeff, Happy Hooligan and George Bungle.

Zero in at sunrise on July 4th,
1935. There stands a squat three-story
Building, white and blue, taller than its width,
Beside it a ten-foot tin Dutchman in blue
Overalls, Falstaff-sized. On the east and west,
Just under the roof, two twenty-foot red fans
Turn slowly in the dawn, above lettering
Like the Declaration of Independence,

Which reads, "The Old Dutch Mill," and just below,
The legend, "We have been laying for you."

Above the shingled roof, two-thirds of a flag
Have clearly flapped through several years of storms.
Back from the road on a ridge of sandy hills
Where arrowheads still lie, are four old barns.
The Mill is surrounded by a Midget
Golf Course and twenty cherry trees whose trunks
Are whitewashed to the lower branches. Jammed
Between these a deserted, screened-in lunch stands
Pictures a girl wearing mainly hip boots, pirate hat
And sword, saying,"Yo ho ho, and a bottle of rum."

Near her lies, snoring under a cherry tree,
An aged airedale resembling William Wordsworth;
His name is Patrick Henry. On the sand hill
Nearest Five Mile Road stands the house of Clyde,
Where Bentleys have lived for a hundred years.
Around it wander ducks, geese, cats, Plymouth Rocks,
White Leghorns, Rhode Island Reds. From its windows
Can be seen Clyde's American flags, on sticks,
Lining Five Mile Road to the River Rouge,
Which winds through woods 3 miles from the Detroit limits.

My father grew up here in the 1880's.
In those barns lived the fairies who had followed
His mother from Ireland in a sailing ship:
They gave no end of trouble to the cows.
Now all's idyllic; the crows flap peacefully
Above the cornfields and the comic signs.
Yet, before the last skyrockets have burst
In the warm Michigan sky this coming night,
Uncle Clyde will meet his Armageddon.
At 8 A.M. our narrative begins.

Canto 2.
An antique Marmon, followed by blue smoke
All the way from Middlebelt, pulled into
The Mill's driveway, just as Clyde had started
Down the sand hill, doing a modified jig
And singing "We will dance the hootchie-kootchie";
He quickly shifted to a limp, holding his head
And groaning musically through the cherry trees.
His nephew, aged sixteen, emerged from the Marmon
After the smoke had cleared. "Hello, Uncle Nell.
Oh baby! A Roman candle just went off in my head."

He rubbed his forehead as though simonizing
His 1929 Pontiac. "I haven't slept
Over 20 minutes since June. I figure
I have a fractured skull, leukemia,
Pneumonia, and a broken leg, not to mention
Piles a foot long." He noticed a mallard drake
Climbing a duck near the refreshment stand,
Seized the creature and hurled it some distance.
"And stay off of Josephine, you big green bastard,"
He said, hobbling off to open the Mill.

"I had sherry for breakfast, to kill off a few germs,"
Clyde added, groaned, and flicked on the lights,
"Also a slice of C. F. Smith's swiss cheese.
I bought 3 pounds, and that dirty son of a sea cook
Sold me a good pound and a half of hole."
We stood surrounded by egg bins, as by rocks
On the seacoast, or by the Milky Way:
Eggs in twelve sizes, duck eggs, pullet eggs,
Goose eggs, double yolkers, brown, and cracked.
He pulled some sandpaper from his hip pocket.

"There's no time to horse around, Nell, old man.
Sandpaper every egg in twenty minutes,
Get every speck of blood, manure, and general

Corruption, then fill up the beer coolers."
I sandpapered beneath the constant gaze
Of Ty Cobb, whose enormous photograph
Filled the wall back of the cash register.
Since he was 18, Clyde had dressed like Cobb,
Come slowly to resemble him, and still held
The base-stealing record for Plymouth High School.

Clyde and I bought eggs at a hundred farms
From Milan to Dundee, riding in Bosco,
The International truck, whose tail gate read
"We have been laying for you." Pat, the airedale,
Sang Irish duets with Clyde on the clay roads,
Wagging his ragged tail in my face as I drove.
The rest of the eggs came from Mendelson's,
On Joy Road in Detroit. The barns stood empty.
I straightened the shelves full of jugs and jars
Labelled "Sorghum," "Apple Cider" and "Home Made Jam."

Twelve kinds of jam, with brown paper labels,
Filled all one wall, except for Ty Cobb.
Clyde sent me to the Western Market once a month
To buy a truckload, bring it to his kitchen,
Steam off the labels and hand-letter new ones.
He told the customers, "This jam was made
By a widow in Northville, with eight children."
Soon the full staff had arrived: Bertha Snodgrass,
Jim and Bill McQuillan, Dolly McCullough,
Old Dad Marsh, and Great Uncle Ora Chilson.

At nine, the customers began to come:
They streamed as bees into a clover field,
Or flights of geese heading down the Huron;
Like buffalo charging across Montana.
They came from Detroit, out Five Mile Road,
From Brightmoor, Novi, Beech and Inkster,
From Rough And Ready, Rosedale, and Stark,

They came from the Biezk Brothers' Garage,
In Packards, Hupmobiles, Studebakers,
Terraplanes, Pierce-Arrows and Model A's.

About half of Livonia Township came:
Oscar Luttermoser, Madonna Goetschius,
Gooseneck and Horseneck Gaffney, Olive Mullins,
Lightning, on a white horse from Wellwood's Stable,
Boob Wolfram, Pipe Wolfram, Cod Wolfram,
Leonard Gascoyne, E. J. Glass, and Great Uncle Charles
Whose palsied hands guided his old blue Buick
Into a small dune between cherry trees;
They came as June bugs cluster on screen doors
And bang and buzz on Michigan summer nights.

So, while children shot firecrackers among cars
And hurled red devils against the whitewashed stones
That circled the cherry trees, I ran all day
Up and down the sand hills with jugs of milk,
Whipping cream, fresh churned buttermilk, cases
Of Stroh's Bohemian Beer, jam, honey and eggs,
Between the 18 holes of the Midget Golf Course,
Frequently chasing Clyde's black and green drake,
Haile Selassie, from his favorite roost
On the 12th green; I pumped Old Dutch Gas;

Brought fresh dressed fryers down from the steamy barn
Where Old Dad Marsh chopped heads, plucked feathers
And raked out hearts; I slung ten-gallon milk cans
And handed out putters and score cards near the lunch stand.
Clyde moved through the crowd in his clear element,
As Namu the killer whale would leap for a fish
Held by his trainer, and with one swish of tail
Propel himself high out of the water;
So Clyde, with the grace of Ty Cobb fielding a grounder,
Jocularly sold eggs, singing "Sweet Betsy From Pike."

Canto 3.
The sun passed over Clyde's flapping remnant flag
And the always turning, latticed windmill blades,
Away from Detroit, and descended toward Livonia.
Crowds thickened through the long bright afternoon,
Some drawn in by signs saying "New Laid Eggs,
Seventeen cents a dozen," "Take a whirl
With Old Dutch Gas," "Biggest fireworks display
In Wayne County here tonight," and "Our Jersey herd
Is the best in Michigan: this is no bull."
Sometimes as Clyde tied egg cartons up with string,

He and Patrick Henry sang a chorus
Of "My Wild Irish Rose," or "Hullabalooloo,
Don't Bring Lulu," the modulated howls
Of the old airedale counterpointing Clyde
With the skill of long winter nights at the piano,
Where they sat for hours, side by side, on the bench
Full of photographs, sounding like the keening
After a shipwreck on the coast of Ireland.
I had this associated with Clyde's frequent comment,
"Your Aunt Gladys is as nervous as a cat."

Much of the day, there was barely room to move
Along the Mill's oily wooden floors;
Customers milled about with glass jugs,
Bumping into the pool table and beer cases,
The cheese and milk case, cans of maple syrup,
Pyramids of Virginia Dare wine bottles,
As Clyde's cats leaped from level to level
Of egg bins, and Bertha Snodgrass grinned
Like an Airflow Chrysler or a seasoned bullhead
Fresh from the reedy shallows of Orchard Lake.

Above this rose the voice of Uncle Clyde,
Like a hot dog and peanut vendor at Navin Field
Or Lauritz Melchior singing Tristan,

Like the bull elk bugling in the Detroit Zoo,
Which pales Woodward Avenue's raucous horns
And halts the rhinoceros in his moody plod.
"Yes ma'am, every egg was laid in those barns
You see up on the sand hill." "That jam was made
By a widow lady who lives over in Beech
With ten children, her old mother and a dachshund."

"The seventeen cent eggs are laid by pullets.
They're small, but sweet as honey. We also have
Twenty other sizes." "No ma'am, we're too busy
To show you the chicken barns today."
"Nell, old boy, run up to the gray barn
And give those chickens some scratch feed and mash.
I want their crops the size of baseballs." "Say,
You ought to see the Northville Hornets play
Phoenix Lake on Sunday. Boob, Pipe, and Cod
Wolfram play the outfield for Northville,

And they're each the spitting image of Babe Ruth."
"Come back for the fireworks. Those old sand hills
Will look like Bunker Hill." Against these comments,
I recalled Clyde setting grass fires for miles around,
Especially on B.E. Taylor's land,
And his telling farmers along the Raisin River
Near Azalea, "This truck is one of a fleet
I have, buying eggs from farms in four states."
Now, sunflowers by the tin Dutchman began to fold
As night settled over Livonia Township.

Canto 4.
And night settled over the black raspberry bushes
In the woods half a mile behind the sand hills,
And over Lake Como, where the caretaker's bulldog
Chased Bruce Haines off the dam at the deep end,
And the River Rouge and Elm Creek, full of cat-tails,
Bull-frogs and minnows, where it came winding
From Elm Woods with its snakes and black-eyed Susans,
Past the house where I was born and still lived,
And night settled over Clyde's five hundred flags
And the rum girl, dressed in her pirate boots,

And night settled on the remaining Model-T's,
And horses and buggies, and on the Pere Marquette
Railroad and hoboes walking its double tracks,
And on the cupola bell-tower of Elm School,
And on Charley White, zigzagging well-oiled
Down Schoolcraft Road, and on Buck St. Clair's
Racks of skunk skins, and on muskrats and jays
And pastures of Holsteins where now a city stands,
And night settled on the deserted hut
Of Frank Burr the hermit, with its photograph

Of Calvin Coolidge surrounded by nude women,
And on Stan Hayes' White Star Gas station, Clyde's
Competitor, and Patrick Henry's birthplace
In Beech near the railroad tracks, and settled over
The sand hills where my father as a boy
Between chores recited the Odyssey in Greek
And grew up to become an English teacher
In Chillicothe, Golden, and Cripple Creek;
And Clyde came forth with fireworks from the Mill
With an expression like Ty Cobb stealing home.

Then for an hour Clyde shot off skyrockets
And Roman candles, each one bursting its storm
Of light above the dunes, the arrowheads,

The cars parked every which way among holes
Of the Midget Golf Course, the great empty barns,
Each burst illuminating the shredded flag
On the Mill's top; Clyde filled the Milky Way
And the Big Dipper with seven skyrockets
At a time, moved mightily with his matchbox
Like Orion among the constellations.

And the white, orange and green sulphurous flashes
Lit up Lightning on his patient white horse,
And Great Uncle Ora, who stood like Mt. Rushmore
Beside the tin Dutchman, and Rube Whitehead,
And Patrick Henry, who was following Clyde
From fuse to fuse. And as the Northern Lights
Send mighty impulses climbing to the zenith,
So Clyde, in a gathering cadenza, running
In his flapping, egg-stained Old Dutch Mill coat,
Sent more rockets over Livonia Township.

"They'll see this all the way to the Book Cadillac,"
He said. The cherry trees were full of pinwheels,
And Clyde now ran full tilt from tree to tree,
Dodging children, Ethiopian ducks and cats,
Signs and automobiles, lighting fuses,
And forty pinwheels spin their phosphorus circles
Like the Ford Factory transfigured, or else
A traffic jam of Ezekiel's chariots.
Clyde stood like George Washington watching
His silver dollar sail over the Potomac.

Canto 5.
Meanwhile down Five Mile Road, fierce in a Ford,
A grim spirit, a lone driver, growling with anger,
Came zigzagging the dark zones of his zeal,
Lurching from the limits of Livonia,
His bone-house bubbling with Brightmoor booze,
A fume-wafter from the fens of Farmington,

Red-eyed and raucous from Rough And Ready,
Sotted and suspicious, a staggerer from Stark,
Pugnacious and unpleasant, pickled in Plymouth,
So came the arch-fiend, five flags on his radiator.

Back in the Mill, Clyde opened an ice cold case
Of Budweiser, and twenty bottles were tilted
Toward Ty Cobb, or the ceiling, in a toast
To Independence; twenty Adam's-apples
Bobbed above the egg-bins: Rube Whitehead's,
Dolly McCullough's, Clyde's, mine, the McQuillans',
Old Dad Marsh's, Lightning's, and sundry customers'.
Bertha Snodgrass went on selling eggs.
Then stumbled unsteadily over the doorsill
Mankind's foe, a firecracker of pure fury.

"Wheresh that confounded cuss, Clyde Bentley?
Shee here, Clyde, I watched yer sh-shkyrocketsh
Goin' up over that p-poor miserable f-flag.
I've had my eye on that f-flag, Clyde Bentley,
For sheveral yearsh, an' every year it'sh shmaller,
An' now it'sh no b-bigger'n a red bandana.
I'm gonna t-teach you shome reshpect for the f-flag."
So spoke the monster, mumbling in malice,
And pushed Old Dad Marsh into an egg bin,
And threw a double handful of eggs onto the floor.

"Whash Ty Cobb doin' over the cash regishter?
Why ishn't that picture of George Washin'ton?

It oughta be ol' George Washin'ton up there, C-Clyde.
I'm gonna throw thish here goosh egg at Ty C-Cobb."
The joyless creature, juggling a giant egg,
Drew back his fist, as for a throw to first.
Clyde set his Budweiser on the stove, calling
"Wait, you infernal fool, not at Ty Cobb!"
A still, small voice seemed to issue from the wall,
As from a third-base coach, calling "Slide, Clyde, slide."

Uncle Clyde skidded across those smashed eggs
Like a salmon struggling up the Skagit,
Knocked the grim, goose-egged enemy galley west,
With a huge hill of honey-combs on his head
And ten gallons of milk gurgling onto his gizzard.
The Antagonist was out cold, and Clyde
Sat by him, straw hat shoved back on his forehead;
They looked like Sohrab and Rustum in a sea
Of broken eggs. Bertha went for the broom
And mop, Rube Whitehead went for the sheriff.

And the Old Dutch Mill was locked by eleven o'clock;
Uncle Nell chugged home in his decrepit Marmon,
The arch-fiend was lodged in the Livonia jail,
Haile Selassie settled down on the 12th green,
And Clyde and Patrick Henry were alone.
I leave them hobbling up the sand hill,
Singing and howling "The Old Oaken Bucket,"
Below the Big Dipper. The ten-foot tin Dutchman
Smiled steadily in the faint gunpowder smell;
Charred pinwheels spun slowly on the cherry trees.

Seattle: September 1973

NELSON BENTLEY was born in Elm, Michigan. He moved to Seattle in 1952 to teach at the University of Washington, where he is now an Associate Professor of English. He is also the author of *Sea Lion Caves* (Swallow Press, 1966) and *Moose Call* (Jawbone Press, 1977).

IRON MAN OF THE HOH was designed at Copperhead. The type is 10 point Journal Roman, set by Irish Setter, with Hadriano Stone Cut display. 1000 copies are sewn in paper covers. The cloth edition is signed by the author.

NELSON BENTLEY was born in Elm, Michigan. He moved to Seattle in 1952 to teach at the University of Washington, where he is now an Associate Professor of English. He is also the author of *Sea Lion Caves* (Swallow Press, 1966) and *Moose Call* (Jawbone Press, 1977).

IRON MAN OF THE HOH was designed at Copperhead. The type is 10 point Journal Roman, set by Irish Setter, with Hadriano Stone Cut display. 1000 copies are sewn in paper covers. The cloth edition is signed by the author.